Journal Your Life's Journey

A Blank Book Billionaire Creation

27469405R00059

Made in the USA
San Bernardino, CA
13 December 2015